Closing the Trapdoor

The abolition of the death penalty for murder in Britain

David Field

Published by

Dayglo Books Ltd, Nottingham, UK

www.dayglobooks.co.uk

0014-15-0406-01

© David Field 2015

The right of David Field to be identified as the author of this work has been asserted by him in accordance with the Designs and Copyright Act 1988.

Cover artwork & illustrations by
www.valentineart.co.uk

Typeset in Opendyslexic
by Abelardo Gonzales (2013)

Printed by IngramSpark

Distributed by Filament Publishing Ltd, Croydon

This book is subject to international copyright and may not be copied in any way without the prior written permission of the publishers.

Foreword

In 1965, Britain formally abolished the death penalty for murder.

In the decade before that, there were three infamous murder trials. After each verdict an allegedly unjust hanging occurred. These hangings fuelled the arguments of the campaigners for abolition.

Of all the mechanical methods of execution, 'death by hanging' carries with it nightmarish visions of highwaymen, traitors and cut-throats.

In post-war Britain, increasing numbers of humane observers were recoiling from the idea of capital punishment.

Those who took the time to inform themselves of how it was done often wished they had remained ignorant.

Judged by any standard, judicial execution is a cold-blooded and bureaucratic matter.

By 1950, it had become almost a science. The public hangman – known as "the public executioner" – was a highly skilled and experienced technician.

What, exactly, was his job?

Closing the Trapdoor

CHAPTER 1 – The Public Executioner

Hanging involved having the condemned prisoner stand on a trapdoor above a void and placing a specially knotted rope around their neck.

The hangman was provided with a printed Home Office instruction manual and all the equipment essential for the job.

The process was based on calculations. It began with the hangman noting the prisoner's height and weight. Armed with this information he would calculate the necessary length of the 'long drop' through the trapdoor.

This measurement would ensure "hyper-flexion of the neck". Hyper-flexion means bending a part of the body – in this case the neck – beyond the normal limit.

When the condemned prisoner reached the terminal point of the drop, hyper-flexion occurred. This would sever the spinal cord, destroy the phrenic nerve and breathing would stop.

The Home Office instruction manual reads, to modern eyes, unnervingly like a guide to constructing an item of flat-pack furniture. It contains lines such as "Obtain a rope from Execution Box B making sure that the splice at each end is un-cracked by previous use".

It also instructs the reader to "Find the required drop from the Official Table of Drops making allowance for age and physique."

The weight of the prisoner dictated the length of the drop. The manual gave a scale which ran (in modern terms) from 2.5 metres for a prisoner weighing 54 kilos or less, down to 1.5 metres for those who weighed over 90 kilos on the day before their execution.

The day before the real thing, a test drop would be made using a sandbag of the same weight as the prisoner. Prior to this, the executioner would take a sneaky peek at the condemned man to confirm his apparent height and build.

Even the ceremonials were dictated by Home Office protocols. In London, the 'drop' would occur at 9 am. Elsewhere in the country, at prisons in which executions were authorised, it was 8 am.

Shortly before the specified time a small group would assemble outside the condemned cell. This was a room adjoining the execution room.

By this time, the prisoner would be dressed in their own clothes. They would have been attended by a priest and a doctor. The doctor's function was usually no more than the administration of a glass of brandy to steady the prisoner's nerves.

The hangman would enter the condemned cell and fasten the condemned person's hands behind their back with a leather strap. The hangman would then hasten back to the trapdoor to ensure that all was as it should be, while the doctor and priest escorted (sometimes half-carried) the prisoner out to the drop-site.

Once standing on the trapdoor, supported on either side by a prison officer, the prisoner's ankles were strapped. Then the hangman put the noose around their neck, and a white hood over their head.

The trapdoor would be opened with the minimum of delay, and it would all be over.

An official notice would be displayed outside the prison, confirming that the law had taken its course. Once a post-mortem had taken place, a brief inquest would be conducted. The cause of death would be certified as "Injuries to the central nervous system consequent upon judicial hanging".

At least the spectacle was no longer conducted in public. The only crowds waiting outside the place of execution would be the shattered relatives and the vocal protestors. By 1950 these protestors had become an increasingly vociferous force to be reckoned with.

CHAPTER 2 – Timothy John Evans

Timothy John Evans was executed in 1950.

A judgment handed down by the High Court in November 2004 declared that: "The conviction of Timothy Evans is now recognised to have been one of the most notorious, if not the most notorious, miscarriages of justice."

Eighty years previously, in November 1924, Timothy Evans had been born in Merthyr Tydfil, South Wales. He never knew his father, who left the family before Timothy was born. Timothy had an older sister, Eileen, When his mother remarried he gained a half-sister, Maureen, and the family moved to London.

By then, the difficulties which the teenage Timothy was to experience were all too obvious. He was a late speaker as a young child and a slow learner at school.

At the age of eight, an accident left him with a foot injury. This caused continued absences from school, and also limited his future employment opportunities.

He suffered low self-esteem and a limp. Timothy began inventing stories about himself. At times he had difficulty in separating the truth from fiction. This was to prove unfortunate in his later dealings with the police.

One of his more exaggerated claims, for example, was that he was the son of an Italian count. He was actually a failed painter and decorator, a failed coalminer, working as a low-paid van driver, with an IQ of 70.

His chosen bride, Beryl, was five years his junior, and was no brighter than he was. Within a few short months of marriage, Beryl was pregnant with their first child. Their daughter, whom they christened Geraldine, was born in October 1948.

They had to move out of Timothy's mother's house where they had been living. They rented a place of their own. The cramped, top floor flat was no more than a bedroom-cum-kitchen without the luxury of even a lounge. The address was number 10, Rillington Place, in London's Notting Hill.

If that address seems chillingly familiar, it is for a very good reason. A certain John Reginald Christie was already living there with his wife, in the ground floor flat. It was a seedy, decaying, narrow Victorian terraced slum.

The address would soon become infamous due to Christie's macabre activities there. So much so that the local council re-named the street in an effort to deter sightseers.

But when the Evans family moved into the top floor flat they had no reason to be worried.

Their ground floor neighbour seemed a quiet, unassuming man, a former postal worker.

They had enough problems, anyway. Timothy earned a low wage, and Beryl was not very good at managing. Not much money remained anyway, after his frequent visits to the pub.

His drinking and limited life-skills, her poor housekeeping, and their constant poverty, led to frequent 'domestics'. Their rows were audible throughout the entire building. Sometimes Timothy would knock Beryl around. When she fell pregnant again, matters were at desperation point.

Like many a post-war family living under such pressures, abortion suggested itself as a solution.

However, abortion was against the law in those days, so it had to be an illegal one.

Their unassuming, obliging, downstairs neighbour, Mr Christie, offered to take care of things. He showed them a St John's Ambulance Brigade handbook which they took to be a medical textbook. They were impressed, and reassured.

Next day, Timothy went off to work as usual.

According to what he subsequently told the police – during his second interview – he came home from work to be told by Christie that Beryl was dead.

Christie said he had arranged for fourteen-month-old Geraldine to be looked after by a local family. Christie advised Timothy that his best course of action would be to sell his few, meagre possessions and leave town.

CHAPTER 3 – The Metropolitan Police

Evans did everything that Christie suggested. However, some inner urging prompted him to walk into a police station in his home town of Merthyr Tydfil.

He announced that his wife had, against his advice, taken some pills supplied by a stranger. He had come home to find her dead. He had hidden her body in a drain with a heavy manhole cover in the garden of Number 10. He said he had entrusted their daughter to the care of another family.

At this stage he was adamant that (a) he had not killed Beryl, and (b) that he had acted alone in disposing of her body.

The Merthyr Tydfil police informed the Metropolitan Police in London, and they quickly disproved this scenario. It took three burly constables to lift the heavy manhole cover. There was no body underneath.

When Evans was told this, he changed his story. He now told the police that it had been Christie who had caused Beryl's death while attempting to procure her abortion. It had been Christie who had disposed of her body.

It was also Christie who had arranged child-care for baby Geraldine.

The Metropolitan Police returned to Number 10, and conducted a search. That search must surely be one of the most totally inept police searches on record.

If they had looked more carefully at what was propping up the back garden fence, they might, perhaps, have identified the object as a human thigh bone.

If they had dug, they would not have needed to go down very far to discover more human remains. This should have aroused suspicions that this was no ordinary garden.

However, they did not look; they did not dig.

The only consequence of the bungled police

search was that Timothy Evans was brought back to London. The police had found a stolen briefcase in his now empty flat.

His ground floor neighbour, Reggie Christie, had told the police that Evans was a known liar, and probably mad.

Evans then gave the police a third version of events. This time, he said that he had helped Christie carry Beryl's body upstairs to his own flat.

Someone in authority in the Met, with actual experience of searching crime scenes, suggested that they search again.

Outside was a small structure that was politely referred to as a 'wash house'. In reality, this was a toilet – the only toilet available for all the tenants of the crumbling residence. It was locked. Inside, the police found the body of Beryl Evans wrapped in several cloths. Under a pile of wood, inside the cramped space, police also found the body of baby Geraldine.

During his fourth interview, Evans was advised of the finding of the two bodies. It must have been his first realisation that his daughter was also dead. He was told that they had both been strangled.

He was asked if he had been responsible, to which he allegedly responded "yes, yes."

There was a great deal of speculation in the months and years that followed as to how genuine this confession had been.

It was made by a man of low IQ, in police custody, without the benefit of legal advice. It was made immediately after being told of the death of his baby daughter.

He later signed a more detailed confession. Some people later argued that the words attributed to him in this confession were not his own. They believed the police had compiled an account of what had happened from the facts known to them at the time.

Evans was a poorly educated man who could only just sign his own name. Critics said he had merely signed on the proverbial dotted line to this version of events.

There was also a suggestion that Evans had

confessed in order to protect Christie. He regarded Christie as his friend. Others believed Evans had been threatened by the officers interrogating him.

Whatever its motivation, this fourth and final statement was in stark contrast to his previous explanations of events.

It was to prove – literally – fatal.

CHAPTER 4 – A Crucial Witness

The police now appeared to put on blinkers. First of all, the police ignored an unpleasant and inconvenient truth. If Evans' confession was correct, then the bodies had been in the 'wash house' (toilet) for several days. But nobody had complained about the smell.

Mrs Christie confirmed, in a statement, that she had been in and out of there on two dozen occasions since Evans' departure from London. However, by the date of the trial her evidence had been 'adjusted'. Mrs Christie now claimed that she never used the 'wash house' once during the relevant time.

At the trial, even Evans' counsel missed the point. The 'wash house' was the only toilet. He failed to comment upon the seemingly astounding capacity of Mrs Christie's bladder.

Then there were the statements made by carpenters who had been working at the house. On the day on which Evans claimed to have left the bodies of his wife and baby in the 'wash house', the workmen were using it all day.

Not only that, but the wood under which baby Geraldine's body had been hidden had a particular significance which was not mentioned.

One of the carpenters had pulled up some floor boards in Christie's flat and had given this wood to Christie.

But this had happened a full eight days after Evans 'confessed' to using that wood to conceal the body. And Evans claimed that immediately after concealing the body he left London for Wales.

Then there was the mystery of the workman's timesheet for the day in question. The timesheet was confiscated from his employer's files by the investigating police officers. It was never returned. This workman – a crucial witness – was not called to testify at Evans' trial.

CHAPTER 5 – An Appointment Kept

Evans' trial opened in January 1950. The Crown prosecutor was Mr Humphreys. Remember his name – it will appear in future chapters in this book.

Evans was accused of the murder of his wife Beryl and his daughter Geraldine.

Mr Humphreys learned that defence counsel planned to seek a lesser charge of manslaughter, on the grounds of 'provocation'.

Mr Humphreys pressed for a charge of murder, but only relating to baby Geraldine. At the age of fourteen months she could have done nothing more provocative than soil her nappy.

Baby Geraldine's body was found in the same place, on the same day, as her mother's.

Because the two deaths were so closely connected, Mr Humphreys was permitted to present evidence relating to Beryl's death.

The star witness for the Crown was undoubtedly 'Reggie' Christie. He laid great emphasis on the frequent, and occasionally violent, quarrels between the couple upstairs.

And he flatly denied having offered to procure Beryl's abortion.

Evans, for his part, performed poorly and unconvincingly in the witness box. There was damning content in the three different and incriminating stories he had given to the police. There was also his alleged confession.

On the third day of the trial, the jury took only forty minutes to find him guilty of the murder of his daughter, Geraldine.

Therefore, on 9 March 1950, in Pentonville Prison, Evans duly kept his appointment with the public executioner. To the very end, Evans told anyone who would listen that "Christie done it."

But Christie shrugged off the accusation.

Then, three years later, a new tenant moved into Christie's old flat. He made a gruesome discovery. Human remains were found in a kitchen recess. This time the police searches were more thorough.

The body of Christie's wife was found beneath the floorboards. He was charged with her murder.

Eventually Christie admitted to the murders of seven women. He had suffocated them in the course of his hobby of choice – raping victims while they were approaching the point of death.

One of those women was Beryl Evans. She had thought Christie was giving her a sedative prior to her abortion. Instead, he killed her.

At that time, domestic gas was coal gas which was potentially lethal if inhaled.

Christie suffocated his victims with gas, using a tube attached to the kitchen gas supply.

Christie pleaded insanity, but to no avail. In July 1953 Christie met the same fate as Evans, on the same gallows, in the same prison, and at the hands of the same executioner.

The hangman was no doubt acutely aware of the unjust thing he had been obliged to do to Evans three years earlier.

When Christie was standing on the trapdoor, he complained that his nose was itching. The hangman is reputed to have responded with the words: "It won't bother you for long."

CHAPTER 6 – Postscript to Timothy Evans

Evans' remaining family launched a campaign to clear his name, following Christie's confession to the murder of Beryl Evans.

In fact, Evans had gone to the gallows for the murder of his baby daughter Geraldine, not his wife Beryl. It was a technical quibble that Christie never admitted to that crime.

In any case, the 'establishment' was unwilling to admit that a man had been unjustly hanged.

In 1948 the then Home Secretary had claimed that there was "no practical possibility" of an innocent man being judicially executed.

The waters got even murkier within weeks of Christie's conviction. An enquiry concluded that Evans had been guilty of the murder of his wife as well as his daughter. This was based on the fact that the two murders had been carried out by the same person.

This enquiry also found that Christie had only been trying to prove his claim of insanity by admitting to killing Beryl Evans.

This enraged those who believed in Evans' innocence. The campaign never ceased and in 1965 a High Court Justice chaired a second enquiry.

This handed down an even more confusing conclusion. It said that while Christie had murdered Geraldine (for which Evans had hanged), it was "more probable than not" that Evans had killed Beryl.

However, this was sufficient to persuade the then Home Secretary to recommend a posthumous pardon to Evans, with which Her Majesty graciously complied.

The timing of this pardon coincided almost exactly with the suspension of the death penalty for murder, about which more is written below.

But there was one more controversy awaiting the Evans family. Hanged criminals were buried in an unmarked grave at the prison where they were executed. The granting of the pardon cleared the way for Timothy's remains to be exhumed from his prison grave and reinterred wherever the family chose.

Tomothy's mother arranged for a burial plot in a cemetery in west London and for a Catholic funeral to be held for her son. This was to take place in conditions of utter secrecy. The family wished to avoid a media circus.

However, the family solicitor found out that the press had leaked the story. In a desperate attempt to protect the family from any press intrusion, he took action.

He arranged for a 'decoy' cortege to leave Pentonville Prison for the west London cemetery with a dummy coffin in the hearse. Meanwhile, the real coffin containing Timothy Evans' body was taken to a cemetery in east London. His mother and sister travelled in the real funeral cortege. Timothy was laid to rest in their presence.

When the media found out what had happened, they got their own back by laying siege to Timothy's mother's house.

The matter was the subject of a question in the House of Commons.

An M.P. claimed that, in respect of Timothy Evans and his family, "we, as a nation, have been guilty of a most terrible miscarriage of justice".

It is difficult not to agree with him.

CHAPTER 7 – Derek William Bentley

Derek William Bentley was hanged in 1953.

"Let him have it, Chris". In written form, those words are strictly neutral. Even when spoken, they require 'context' in order to give them meaning.

For example, if they were spoken by an encouraging mother to her small son, they could be a gentle urging to hand Granddad his birthday present.

On a rooftop, late at night, surrounded by police intent on making an arrest, when uttered to a companion who is armed with a Colt .45, they could be taken as an incitement to shoot.

Derek Bentley would later claim that he did not utter these words. Or if he did, they were intended to urge his companion, Christopher Craig, to hand over the gun peacefully. Neither version saved him from the gallows less than three months later.

Like Timothy Evans before him, Derek Bentley had a low IQ – 77 in his case. He was also epileptic. Like Evans, Bentley was poorly educated.

He had an estimated mental age of 11 when he was hanged at the age of 19.

All men were routinely conscripted into the armed forces in the early nineteen fifties but Bentley was rejected as "mentally substandard".

He even managed to fail as a dustman for the local council. He was demoted to street sweeping until he was dismissed from that job for "unsatisfactory performance" two months later.

Many young men in his position took to crime, and Bentley was no exception. He was reported as being "outside parental control". After he was caught warehouse breaking, he was committed for a stretch in a youth detention centre.

The educational psychologist there gave a report that reads ominously, in view of subsequent events. He stated that Derek was dim enough to be the one caught if there was trouble and the brighter boys fled. Derek was "never violent", but instead was "bullied and easily led."

When he returned home from youth custody, Derek rapidly became "easily led" by Christopher Craig.

Craig was three years younger than Bentley. Craig's older brother had already graduated into the world of local crime.

Chris Craig himself was obsessed with American gangster movies. He modelled himself on the street thugs depicted by his screen idols.

He must have cut quite a glamorous figure in the streets of South London.

Bentley was shy, introverted, uneducated and friendless. He was flattered when Chris began to show an interest in him. He began 'hanging out' with Craig, despite warnings from his family, who were concerned.

On the evening of 2 November, 1952, the two youths set out together. They turned their criminal attentions to a warehouse in Croydon, just south of London.

Bentley was proudly carrying in his pocket a sheath knife and a knuckle-duster Craig had given him.

Craig, for his part, had in his pocket a sawn-off Colt .45 and a supply of modified bullets.

There is some doubt as to whether or not Bentley was aware that Craig had a gun before they set out.

When they reached the warehouse they climbed the perimeter gate and shimmied up an external drainpipe towards the roof.

However, they had been spotted from across the road by a nine-year-old girl, whose parents alerted the police. One of the most controversial crimes of the century was about to unfold.

What happened next was contested at the trial. However, the general consensus seems to have been that the first police officer onto the roof was a plain-clothes detective called Fairfax.

Craig and Bentley had initially hidden

themselves behind the lift-housing. Bentley made a run for it, and was grabbed by Detective Fairfax. He managed to break free, temporarily.

Craig then produced his gun. Someone (believed to have been Detective Fairfax) said "Don't be stupid, son – put the gun down". Then Bentley is alleged to have uttered the words "Let him have it, Chris".

Craig fired, hitting Detective Fairfax in the shoulder. Despite this, the officer was able to regain his grip on Bentley. Instead of taking advantage of the situation to break free, Bentley accepted that he was being detained.

He devoted his efforts to warning the officer that Craig was armed, and had a good supply of ammunition. Significantly, he made no effort to use either the knife or the knuckle-duster in order to regain his freedom.

Other police reinforcements piled onto the roof. Some were armed, and Craig let fly a volley of shots.

Some *fifteen minutes later,* uniformed P.C. Sidney Miles came into view. Craig shot him right between the eyes, before running out of ammunition and jumping off the roof.

CHAPTER 8 – A Common Design

Craig broke his back in the fall. He was taken into custody and to the local hospital. Bentley 'came quietly'. On his journey in the police car he is alleged to have told officers, of Chris Craig, "I knew he had a gun but I didn't think he'd use it."

His defence in court was that his precise words had been "I *did not* know Chris had a gun".

There is a world of difference between those two statements – especially in the context of 'action in concert' which was the main plank of the Crown's case against Bentley for the murder of P.C. Miles.

They faced a joint trial barely six weeks later at the Old Bailey. The murder of a police officer could not have occurred at a worse time for the two young men.

The early nineteen-fifties was the start of a period of sustained economic prosperity in Britain, following the privations of the Second World War.

But it brought with it an outbreak of youth lawlessness which was American influenced. In particular, this resulted in confrontations between groups of police and gangs of armed thugs.

Four police officers had been murdered in the line of duty the previous year. The British public wished to enjoy their new-found luxuries free of the threat of 'cosh-boy' gangs.

Public opinion is usually expressed in (and frequently formed by) the pages of the popular press. The day after the rooftop incident, the Daily Mail trumpeted a lead story about it.

The story described a "Chicago Gun Battle in London". It featured "gangsters with machine guns" who had taken on two hundred police officers. Thirty of these officers were armed with service revolvers. "Hand to hand battles" had ensued before "the two gunmen" had been subdued.

The same newspaper, among others, was to

swing its published opinion through one hundred and eighty degrees after the trial. It then joined the cry for the abolition of the death penalty.

But for the time being, it bayed loudly for the blood of those gangsters. They had taken the life of a police officer; a father of two who was only doing his job in protecting the public.

Politicians are sensitive. In order to demonstrate that the Government was taking the matter seriously, the trial was entrusted to the then Lord Chief Justice of England.

This man was known by many who had appeared before him as "the hanging judge".

Counsel for the Crown was once again Mr Humphreys. He was fresh from his triumph in sending Timothy Evans to his earthly rewards. As if that were not bad enough for Bentley, his own defence counsel is reputed to have said: "I think the little bastard should hang, don't you?"

It was the Crown's 'theory of the case' that Craig and Bentley had entered into 'a common design' to resist lawful arrest by violence. This required that they prove three facts:

(a) that Bentley knew that Craig had a gun *before* they jointly set about resisting arrest by the shooting of P.C. Miles;

(b) that Bentley had not 'withdrawn' from that common design at the time when the officer was shot;

(c) that Bentley 'egged on' Craig at the

crucial moment, prior to the latter firing the fatal shot.

While the Crown case against Craig could not have been any clearer, the case against Bentley was much less so.

CHAPTER 9 – Fifteen Minutes

The Crown might have anticipated some difficulty in proving its case. There were questions.

Firstly, did Bentley know that Craig was carrying the gun? The only 'evidence' came from a disputed statement inside the police car on the way into custody.

Even if the police version was believed, the fact was that Bentley did not try to get away once he had been restrained by Detective Fairfax.

His only subsequent contribution to the proceedings was the equally contested phrase "Let him have it, Chris". Bentley had called this out to Craig, *immediately after* Detective Fairfax had advised Craig to put down the gun.

Fifteen minutes elapsed before Craig shot P.C. Miles. Could it really be said that this shooting had been encouraged by Bentley?

Initially, there was some doubt whether Bentley should even be deemed mentally 'fit to stand trial'.

The Government's Chief Medical Officer sought a psychiatric assessment of Bentley. The report was that Bentley was "almost borderline retarded". Conveniently, this was taken to mean that Bentley was not legally 'insane' and the trial was allowed to proceed. The jury never heard evidence of the psychiatric assessment

The pathologist who carried out the post-mortem on P.C. Miles, was able to advise the court that no bullet was found in the deceased's head.

However, he was not asked to confirm the calibre of the bullet. If he had, it could have been inconvenient for the Crown. The pathologist estimated that the bullet which killed P.C. Miles had been between .32 and .38 calibre. It had been fired from some two to three metres away.

Craig's gun could not possibly have fired a bullet of as small a calibre as even .38.

Craig had fired from twelve metres away.

At that distance, with a Colt .45, he would have been very lucky to hit any part of P.C. Miles, let alone put a shot between his eyes.

One can understand the Crown's anxiety to suppress the information regarding a .32 sized wound. That was the calibre of the Webley automatics used by the police that night.

A discharged .32 bullet was found on the roof afterwards. This suggested a possible death by 'friendly fire' from a police weapon.

The judge appeared to be entirely on the side of the prosecution. When the two accused tried to tell their stories, he made several irritated interruptions. In his summing up to the jury, he left them in no doubt as to what they should conclude.

With regard to whether or not Bentley knew Craig had a gun, his Lordship is on record as saying:

"Because I sit on the Bench and you sit in the jury-box it is not necessary that we leave our common sense at home," he began.

"Can you suppose for a moment," he continued, "especially when you have heard Craig say that he carried a revolver for the purpose of boasting and making himself a big man . . . that he would not have told his pals he was out with that he had got a revolver?

"Is it not inconceivable," the judge asked, "that Craig would not have told him, and probably shown him the revolver which he had?"

That was not a comment on any evidence

which had actually been heard. It was an invitation to conjecture. It would have been 'over the top' even from Crown Counsel.

Even worse was the way in which his Lordship invited the jury to deal with any discrepancy between the evidence of Bentley, on the one hand, and Detective Fairfax and another officer.

In fact, his Lordship referred, inaccurately, to the "three" officers. In fact only two officers actually testified the Crown's way regarding whether or not Bentley uttered the words: "Let him have it, Chris".

The judge conflated bravery with honesty in his comment on what he called "the most serious piece of evidence against Bentley", that:

". . . . those three officers in particular showed the highest gallantry and resolution; they were conspicuously brave. Are you going to say they are conspicuous liars?

"Do you believe that those three officers have come into the box and sworn what is deliberately untrue?

"Those three officers who on that night showed a devotion to duty for which they are entitled to the thanks of the community?"

Chapter 10 – Burden of Proof

Finally, in a piece of theatricality which would have come better from Crown Counsel (if at all) his Lordship called for the knuckle-duster which Bentley had been carrying. He gave the jury a graphic illustration of how it could be employed against another person. It is worth recording that his Lordship's fingers were too fat for him to put it on.

He then did the same with the sheath knife. He all but invited the jury to take both of them into the jury room with them as a reminder when they came to consider their verdict.

Regarding Bentley's knowledge that Craig was carrying the gun he advised them that:

"You are not bound to believe Bentley if you think the inference and common sense of the matter is overwhelming that he must have known that he had it."

This invited the jury to *disbelieve* Bentley. Of course, they were only entitled to do so if they found the entire Crown's case proved against him 'beyond reasonable doubt'.

His Lordship implied a shifting of the burden of proof back onto the accused when he advised the jury that:

"In this case the prosecution have given abundant evidence for a case calling for an answer."

It was possible to infer from this that once the Crown had produced a credible case, the burden shifted to the accused to disprove it, or face conviction.

The jury had heard only ten hours of evidence in total.

Bentley himself did not assist his cause by his performance in the witness box – how could a grown man with a mental age of eleven?

The only published photograph of him at that time showed him with a defiant sneer and an unlit cigarette dangling carelessly from his lips.

If he looked anything like that in court, he probably appeared every inch the 'cosh-boy' hoodlum that the Crown sought to depict.

That wasn't his counsel's only difficulty. There were Bentley's words immediately before the fatal shot was fired.

And what had Bentley really said, with regard to his knowledge of Craig's gun?

Any attack on the character of a prosecution witness entitled the Crown to fire back by revealing the accused's criminal record. Bentley had 'previous' in generous measure.

And it was an awkward and unpopular matter for the defence, to attack the word of the police officers.

The trial judge had called those officers "conspicuously brave" and gallant.

A hostile attack on law and order heroes would go badly in any appeal for clemency against the death penalty, if Bentley was convicted.

Finally, how could defence counsel invite the jury to conclude that when he said "Let him have it, Chris," Bentley had meant Craig to simply hand over the gun? The essence of Bentley's defence was that he hadn't even said it.

The jury returned two 'Guilty' verdicts after only 75 minutes. However, the judge's satisfaction was tempered by two facts:

(a) Craig could not hang. He was only 16. The statutory age for judicial execution was 18 years.

(b) The jury recommended clemency for Bentley. The issue of clemency was a matter for the Home Office, not for the judge.

His Lordship had only one course available to him. Craig was sentenced to be detained 'during Her Majesty's Pleasure'. In other words, an indeterminate sentence.

Bentley was sentenced to hang.

CHAPTER 11 – No Mitigating Circumstances

The ever-fickle public opinion now swung behind Bentley. The reason was obvious, if somewhat emotive.

The man who actually fired the gun was only going behind bars for a long time.

The man who had done nothing but, arguably, try to talk him out of it, was to be dispatched on the end of a rope.

Where was the logic, or justice, of that?

Almost immediately, a campaign was launched, led by Bentley's family. The aim was to have the death sentence overturned.

There was another good legal argument against hanging Bentley. This seems not to have featured in the debates at the time.

Under the law as it was, a child aged under eight was deemed by law incapable of forming the necessary 'criminal intent' to commit a crime.

The law did not, therefore, allow a child under eight even to be *charged* with a crime. They were not regarded as having the necessary 'cognitive', or reasoning, skills to form an intention to commit a criminal act.

Bentley, as we know, had a mental age of

eleven. Even at the age of eleven the law required proof that the offender truly knew the difference between right and wrong before they could be convicted.

There was an argument that was not made. A person aged eight – only three years below Bentley's mental age – could not be considered criminally liable.

Where was the humanity in sending to the gallows someone mentally only three years above the age of eight?

And was it reasonable for Bentley to be held liable for the interpretation that Craig put on his words?

Finally, why should Craig escape the noose

because he was sixteen, when Bentley was functionally only eleven?

No wonder the authorities refused to allow the psychiatric assessment of Bentley to be published until it was too late to have any effect.

Bentley's lawyers had obviously lodged an appeal against conviction and sentence. They can hardly have been surprised when it was knocked back on January 11, 1953.

The judges who sat on the appeal were in effect being asked to conclude that their 'boss', the Lord Chief Justice, had got it wrong.

But the matter would not go away. Relentless lobbying by the relatives attracted the sympathy of a great number of supporters.

People famous and otherwise put their names to the petition which was passed hastily around the nation.

The clock continued ticking for the young man now in Wandsworth Prison, counting down the days to his execution,

The family lost no time in making an application to the Home Secretary for mercy. The Home Secretary consulted with the trial judge, who had passed on the jury's recommendation for clemency. He secretly believed that the pardon would be granted.

He advised the Home Secretary that he "could find no mitigating circumstances."

CHAPTER 12 – A Full Posthumous Pardon

The issues were, of course, complex.

On the one hand were the humane principles already mentioned. On the other hand was the need to display a firm resolve against lawlessness.

Plus the fact that the murder victim had been a police officer acting in the course of his duties.

While the Home Secretary was considering what to do, a number of M.P.s demanded that the matter be debated in the House. They were advised by the Speaker that a debate could only be held once the sentence had been carried out!

It was now the night before Bentley's scheduled hanging. Over 200 M.P.s signed a letter calling on the Home Secretary to do the decent thing and grant a reprieve. Amid howls of protest, the reprieve was refused.

During the final hours before the sentence was due to be carried out, crowds began massing outside Wandsworth Prison.

There were an estimated three hundred people there shortly after 9 am on 28 January 1953, when the official death notice was pinned to the prison gates.

The notice was pulled down, torn and burned by the crowd chanting "Murder!" Two people were subsequently convicted of malicious damage to the death notice.

The night before his death, Bentley's older sister, Iris, vowed to him that she would never rest until his name had been cleared.

She almost succeeded. His name was cleared, but she died a few months before.

A subsequent Home Secretary rejected a report by the Metropolitan Police themselves. Somewhat embarrassingly, The Met had been forced to conclude that there were "reasonable doubts" regarding the evidence which had led to Bentley's execution.

Iris did, however, live to hear a new Home Secretary publically announce that Bentley should not have hanged.

However, it only went so far as to concede that the death penalty had been inappropriate, not that the conviction itself had been wrong. The campaign continued.

Then, by unanimous judgment, on 30 July 1998 the Court of Appeal overturned Bentley's conviction and granted him a full posthumous pardon.

The then Lord Chief Justice was among those who was forced to concede that the trial judge had been "blatantly prejudiced" in the manner in which he had supervised the trial. He had misdirected the jury whilst at the same time leaning heavily on them to convict.

By this means, Bentley had been denied "that fair trial which is the birthright of every British citizen." He added that the mis-trial was "a matter of profound and continuing regret."

Bentley's sister Iris was instrumental in arranging for her brother's remains to be transferred from his unmarked grave inside the prison grounds to a private plot in Croydon cemetery. Beneath his name on the headstone are the defiant words: "A victim of British justice".

Bentley's grave is just a few yards from where the ashes of P.C. Miles had been scattered all those years previously.

The last word must go to Christopher Craig, who was released from custody after serving only ten years. The day following Bentley's pardon he was quoted in the British press, as stating that: "I am saddened that it has taken those 46 years for the authorities in this country to admit the truth . . . Now at last this case is over."

CHAPTER 13 – Ruth Ellis

Ruth Ellis was hanged in 1955.

This is the third case which evoked a demand for the abolition of the death penalty. This case was in sharp contrast to the first two cases.

Unlike Timothy Evans and Derek Bentley, the girl who grew up as Ruth Neilson had no developmental handicaps. She lived first in Rhyl, in North Wales, then in Basingstoke, and finally central London.

She was in all ways perfectly normal when she took the life of her lover. She shot him outside a public house in a busy street.

Her only handicap was possibly her greatest asset – she was physically very attractive. Her looks were in the 'pin-up girl' style.

Ruth's good looks got her plenty of attention. They brought her plenty of the good things in life. They also indirectly led to her downfall.

She worked as a shop assistant, a factory hand and a waitress in order to feed herself and her baby son, Andy.

But Ruth was tired of her humdrum life. She took to nude modelling. Then she obtained a position as a nightclub hostess in a club in the West End. She left her small son, Andy, for her mother to bring up.

There is little doubt that during this period she engaged in prostitution. Ruth Ellis was what was called in the 1950s a 'tart'.

When she became pregnant by one of her regular clients, she had an illegal abortion. She returned to work with the minimum of delay.

Ruth Neilson became Ruth Ellis in 1950, aged 24. She married George Ellis, a divorced dentist almost twice her age. She had met him through her club work. Not surprisingly, he was always suspicious that she was conducting affairs. He was a violent alcoholic. The marriage was doomed.

Ellis gave him a daughter, Georgina, whom he refused to acknowledge as his. Ruth responded by moving back in with her parents, taking the little girl with her. She drifted back into 'hostessing'.

Three years later, she was installed as the manageress of a nightclub, living in the flat above. The club was patronised by the rich and famous. They made a big fuss of the attractive platinum blonde. One of her regular patrons was a motor racing driver. Through him, Ruth met the man whose death was to result in her own death.

David Blakely was a hard-drinking, former public schoolboy. He liked fast cars and fast women. He was already engaged to someone whom his parents regarded as suitable.

However, within weeks of meeting her, David Blakely was installed in Ruth's upstairs flat. When she became pregnant again, once more she had an illegal abortion.

Ruth was sacked from her club job. She lost the flat that went with it. She moved into an up-market apartment just off Oxford Street that belonged to a wealthy World War Two bomber pilot and became his mistress.

CHAPTER 14 – Easter Weekend

However this did not stop her carrying on a stormy and increasingly violent relationship with David Blakely. First of all he offered to marry her – and she accepted. Then, when she was pregnant again, he caused her to miscarry by punching her violently in the stomach.

Even worse, from Ruth's point of view, Blakely was seeing other women.

Blakely had a friend named Anthony

Findlater. He and Blakely were devoting all their priorities to building a racing car together. Things came to a head over the Easter weekend of 1955. Blakely was staying with Anthony Findlater and his family.

He repeatedly ignored Ruth's phone calls. He refused to keep his promise to meet her. Ruth was convinced that Blakely to carrying on an affair with the Findlaters' new nanny. Building the racing car was just a cover.

What exactly happened that Easter Sunday was the subject of much conjecture. But its sequel was very public.

Ruth knew that Blakely used to drink at the Magdala public house in Hampstead.

She persuaded her World War Two bomber pilot to drive her to Hampstead. Ruth waited outside the pub until Blakely came out. She called out to him but he signed his own death warrant by ignoring her.

To everyone's surprise – and perhaps even her own – she produced a .38 Smith and Wesson revolver. She fired a shot, which missed.

She pursued Blakely around his parked car. She hit him with a second shot which sent him to the pavement. Then she stood over him and discharged the rest of the magazine. One of the shots was from point blank range.

Ruth stood there, seemingly mesmerised by what she had done.

She still had the smoking gun in her hand. She was arrested by an off-duty police officer. He reported hearing her say: "I am guilty. I'm a little confused."

She was taken to Hampstead police station, where she was interviewed at length. She calmly admitted to what she had done. It was noted that she appeared to be perfectly lucid and sober.

She appeared before magistrates the following morning and was remanded to Holloway women's prison to await trial.

During that period, she was subjected to the usual medical tests in the hospital wing. She was kept under constant surveillance, because she was believed to be a suicide risk.

They need not have worried. The results of all the tests were clear – she was sane and 'fit to plead'. She suffered no brain abnormalities, no hallucinations, no delusions.

In fact, nothing to account for her behaviour outside the Magdala pub that Easter weekend.

CHAPTER 15 – The Inevitable Sentence

This must have caused much head-scratching by Ruth's legal team. They were not only seeking some explanation for her actions, but something that in law might constitute a 'defence'.

The most obvious defence available to her at that time seemed to be 'provocation'. This meant being 'provoked' beyond the level of self-restraint expected of an 'ordinary' person. This would have reduced the charge from murder to manslaughter.

The obvious benefit of that would be prison instead of the death penalty if she was convicted.

But Ruth seemed determined to seal her own fate. She refused to depict herself as provoked by Blakeley's persistent rejection.

Her Old Bailey trial opened on 20 June 1955. By coincidence, once again the prosecuting counsel was Mr Humphreys. Ruth's lawyers must have hung their heads and groaned when he asked her:

"Mrs Ellis, when you fired that revolver at close range into the body of David Blakely, what did you intend to do?"

She replied: "It was obvious that when I shot him I intended to kill him."

This statement was delivered calmly and logically.

Ruth was dressed in a black two-piece suit with a white silk blouse. Her hair was freshly bleached and styled. She must have looked every inch like a cool, well-organised private secretary.

She certainly looked a far cry from an emotional, remorseful victim of rejection who had been driven 'over the edge' by her lover's behaviour.

Little wonder that the judge could find no shred of evidence upon which the jury might consider a finding of manslaughter.

In response to this, Ruth's defence counsel

said there was nothing he could say by way of a closing address in his client's favour. Mr Humphreys agreed not to make a closing submission for the prosecution.

His Lordship then firmly directed the jury, as a matter of law, not even to consider the possibility of 'manslaughter on the ground of provocation'.

He added: "This Court is not a court of morals. It is a criminal court and you should not allow your judgement to be swayed, or your minds to be prejudiced because, by to her own admission, she had committed adultery. Or because she was having two persons at different times as lovers. Dismiss these matters wholly from your minds.

"But I am bound to tell you this – that even if you accept every word of Mrs Ellis' evidence, there does not seem to be anything in it which establishes any sort of defence to the charge of murder."

That translates roughly as: "Don't judge her because she's a self-admitted tart. She has sent herself to the gallows with her own mouth."

Fourteen minutes later, the jury returned with the inevitable verdict, and his Lordship passed the inevitable sentence.

CHAPTER 16 – No Reprieve

As the final act of her polite and restrained performance in the dock, when sentence of death was passed upon her, Ruth replied with a dignified "Thank you."

His Lordship was sufficiently impressed to recommend a reprieve, but this fell on the deaf ears at the Home Office. Ruth herself told everyone who promised to petition on her behalf, including her own mother, that she wasn't interested in overturning the verdict.

But that did not deter her solicitor from petitioning the Home Secretary. However, the Home Secretary decided to reject the petition. He did so with words that, with the benefit of hindsight, seem almost prophetic:

"If a reprieve were to be granted in this case, I think that we should have seriously to consider whether capital punishment should be retained as a penalty."

Ruth's reaction was to sack the solicitor who had organised the petition on her behalf.

Ruth's stoicism persisted to the last. Everyone associated with her commented on how calm and unafraid she seemed, as the clock ticked down to the appointed hour.

Her attitude towards the death penalty was grimly Biblical. As she said to her trial solicitor: "A life for a life. Isn't that just?"

She made a somewhat enigmatic statement to her spiritual adviser just prior to her death. She said: "It is quite clear to me that I was not the person who shot him. When I saw myself with the revolver I knew I was another person."

The appointed hour came at 9 am on 13 July 1955. Her female warders, who had been her constant companions for the last weeks of her life, were on the verge of tears. They were all too familiar with the process.

The drop had been set at 2.5 metres. Ruth weighed a mere 47 kg at this point.

Her warders apologised for the fact that Ruth would be obliged to don a pair of heavy calico knickers to preserve her modesty on the drop.

Ruth cheerfully put them on. Then she took off her glasses with the words: "I won't be needing these any more".

Then the warders led her the 4.5 metres from her cell to the gallows, her hands tied behind her. Twelve seconds later, she was dead.

Even if Ruth had been indifferent to her fate, others had not. The crowd outside Holloway Prison on the morning of her execution was estimated at a thousand. Some of them were women with prams, silently protesting that the system had just taken the life of a young mother of two.

However, the near riot which had followed the hanging of Derek Bentley was not repeated. The execution notice remained untouched when it was posted outside the prison gates at 9.18 am, and the crowd dispersed.

CHAPTER 17 – Sad Sequels

Tragedy seemed to dog even Ruth's memory, with a succession of sad sequels.

In 1969, her mother was found unconscious in a gas-filled room. It appeared to have been a suicide attempt. It resulted in her spending the rest of her life without the power of speech.

Ruth's official husband, George Ellis, hanged himself four years after Ruth's death. By that time he had become a hopeless alcoholic.

Her daughter Georgina was three years old when her mother paid the ultimate price. She was adopted, but died of cancer aged 50.

As for Ruth's son, Andy, who was only ten when his mother was judicially executed, his end was arguably the most tragic.

At some stage, Ruth's remains had been reinterred from the nameless hole in the ground in the yard of Holloway Prison into a private plot in a cemetery.

In 1982, her son, Andy, first of all desecrated her headstone. Then he took his own life in his squalid bedsit. He had been battling with schizophrenia and drug addiction.

Later, it emerged that the judge and

prosecuting counsel at Ruth's trial felt great sympathy for her family. The judge had regularly sent money for Andy's support. Mr Humphreys paid for Andy's funeral.

In 2003 the Court of Appeal threw out a request that her conviction be amended to one for manslaughter on the ground of provocation.

This time the argument was the more recently-recognised one of "Battered Woman Syndrome". However, this argument was dismissed as being "without merit".

The Lord Justice who gave the verdict considered the appeal a waste of time. He said:

"We have to question whether this exercise of considering an appeal so long after the event, when Mrs Ellis herself had consciously and deliberately chosen not to appeal at the time, is a sensible use of the limited resources of the Court of Appeal."

CHAPTER 18 – In Society's Name

Three totally different cases.

The pathetic Timothy Evans was hanged for a crime committed by a man he regarded as a friendly neighbour. That man raped and murdered Timothy's wife and killed his baby daughter.

The immature Derek Bentley, who was in the wrong place at the wrong time. The only person who had ever shown him friendship shot a police officer and Derek hanged for it.

Finally Ruth Ellis, upon whom Mother Nature had showered blessings in abundance. Depending upon your viewpoint, Ruth was either the tragic victim of unrequited passion, or a spoiled, attention-seeking tart.

They all had one thing in common. They gave their names to a growing demand for an end to the death penalty.

As the post-war fifties changed into the swinging sixties, there was a new liberal spirit in Britain.

'Rights' of every kind were demanded, and none more so than human rights. It was time to challenge what had been going on for centuries in society's name.

Traditional objections to judicial execution were based on humanity and logic. Now there were the horror stories of Evans, Bentley and Ellis.

One had been wrongly convicted. One should not have been hanged because his crime did not justify it. The third was a young mother of two young children.

Despite this, the death sentence continued in Britain until 1964. True, by that time the number of prisoners reprieved exceeded the number actually hanged.

Sydney Silverman, M.P., and his supporters campaigned against capital punishment. They hoped to put a stop to the death penalty for an experimental period of five years. They believed this would demonstrate that the number of murders did not increase in the absence of hanging.

The Campaign for the Abolition of Capital Punishment gathered momentum. The law finally changed in 1969. Hanging for murder was replaced with a sentence of life imprisonment.

Capital punishment will most probably never return to Britain. The European Union denies membership to any nation with a death penalty on its statute books.

PEOPLE NAMED IN THE BOOK

Chapters 2 – 6   The Evans Case

Timothy Evans — Hanged for murder. Lived in the same house as Christie.

Eileen & Maureen — Sisters of Timothy Evans

Beryl Evans — Timothy Evans' wife

Geraldine Evans — Timothy Evans' daughter

Reggie Christie — Mass murderer

Mrs Christie — Reggie Christie's wife

Mr Humphreys — Crown prosecutor

Chapters 7 – 12   The Bentley Case

Derek Bentley — Hanged for murder. Friend of Christopher Craig

Christopher Craig	Friend of Bentley. Aged 16
Iris	Derek Bentley's sister
Detective Fairfax	Captured Bentley on roof
P.C. Miles	Shot by Craig on roof
Mr Humphreys	Crown prosecutor
<u>**Chapters 13 - 18**</u>	<u>**The Ellis Case**</u>
Ruth Ellis	Hanged for Murder. Shot her lover.
George Ellis	Ruth's husband
Ruth Neilson	Ruth's name before her marriage to George Ellis
Andy	Ruth's son
Georgina	Ruth's daughter

David Blakely	Ruth's lover. Killed by her.
Anthony Findlater	Friend of David Blakely
Mr Humphreys	Crown prosecutor

Chapter 19

Sydney Silverman	Campaigner against capital punishment

www.ingramcontent.com/pod-product-compliance
Lightning Source LLC
Chambersburg PA
CBHW021116080526
44587CB00010B/540